ADVERTISING

Advertisements on the Metropole Hotel, New York City, in 1909. (The Bettmann Archive)

←A FIRST BOOK→

ADVERTISING

by Richard O. Pompian

Illustrated with photographs

Franklin Watts, Inc.
575 Lexington Avenue
New York, N.Y. 10022

SBN 531-00710-3

Copyright © 1970 by Franklin Watts, Inc.
Library of Congress Catalog Card Number: 70-114921
Printed in the United States of America

CONTENTS

ADVERTISING

GET FREE ARCHIE TOYS

IN THESE Post CEREALS

ARCHIE'S CAR

inside Alpha-Bits

AN ARCHIE RECORD

on Super Sugar Crisp*

JUMPIN' ARCHIES

one inside each box of Honeycomb*

ARCHIE RUB-ONS
inside Sugar Rice Krinkles
(*Rub-ons Trademark Hasbro Industries, Inc.)

ARCHIE SKIN RUB-ONS
inside Crispy Critters
(*Rub-ons Trademark Hasbro Industries, Inc.)

GF GENERAL FOODS

LIMITED SUPPLY—IN SPECIALLY MARKED BOXES

© 1969 Archie Comic Publications, Inc.

Advertising is found everywhere in modern American society. It is used by many different kinds of businesses and individuals and is aimed at people of all ages. (The Post Cereals Division of the General Foods Corporation by Benton & Bowles, Inc.)

ADVERTISING IN AMERICAN SOCIETY

Advertising is found everywhere in modern American society. Most of the advertisements you see and hear are in newspapers and magazines and on radio and television. However, these sources account for only a small percentage of the advertising messages you are exposed to. How many advertising messages do you think your mother saw and heard and read today? Would you guess the figures to be 100? 250? 500? One advertising executive has claimed that the average person is bombarded with 1,600 advertising messages each day! If that sounds hard to believe, just think of all the ads you see in one daily newspaper.

Advertising is big business. Many people believe that advertising plays a very important role in promoting our nation's economic growth. In 1968, almost 18 billion dollars was spent on advertising in America. That is about ninety dollars for every man, woman, and child. Some advertisers estimate that American teen-agers alone will spend up to 45 billion dollars in 1970, and much advertising is geared to the teen market. Also in 1968, over six hundred American advertising agencies did 8.9 billion dollars of advertising business in countries outside of the United States.

Thousands of different kinds of businesses, institutions, and individuals in America use advertising. Not only products and services are advertised. Nonprofit organizations, special-interest groups,

3

Peace on earth.

We'll never win a Nobel peace prize, but in our own small way we do what we can.

For instance, arguing over what to watch on one big TV isn't very peaceful.

With little Sony TV's, you can all be together and still watch what you want to watch.

All solid state, they start with the 4" and inch up—5", 7", 8"—to an 11" screen, measured diagonally. There's one with a built-in Digimatic clock.

There's even a Sony color TV with a new color TV system that's a lot better than the old system everyone else uses.

A little Sony...a little peace and quiet...that's little enough to give anyone. **Sony**

An advertising agency may service anywhere from five to fifty advertisers. The Sony Corp. of America, an advertiser, is a client of the Doyle, Dane, Bernbach agency. (Doyle, Dane, Bernbach, Inc.)

and political candidates advertise also. Over forty-eight hundred advertising agencies help these businesses and individuals by creating and producing their advertising. An agency may service anywhere from five to over fifty advertisers, who are called clients.

Advertising agencies also supply thousands of jobs for skilled workers and college graduates. Photographers, printers, actors, fashion illustrators, motion picture producers, and researchers are among the many involved in advertising.

Almost all newspapers, magazines, and radio and television stations support themselves from the money they earn by carrying advertising. Over 5 billion dollars is spent each year on newspaper advertising alone. Without advertising you would have to pay more for your newspaper. Many newspapers would go out of business. Perhaps you think America could do without some of its 1,752 daily and 7,731 weekly newspapers or its 3,000 magazines. But many people would not like to see their favorite periodicals vanish.

Radio and television would also be different without advertising income. Today there are over five thousand radio and television stations in America. In many countries with little or no advertising there are only one or two radio and television stations.

The United States Post Office earns about 2½ billion dollars each year from the postage spent on advertising sent through the mail.

Advertising means different things to different people. Experts have been arguing for years about the definition. Two of the early popular definitions were "advertising is news" and "advertising is salesmanship in print." As advertising grew more complex, so did the definitions. Some said advertising was informing and teaching

5

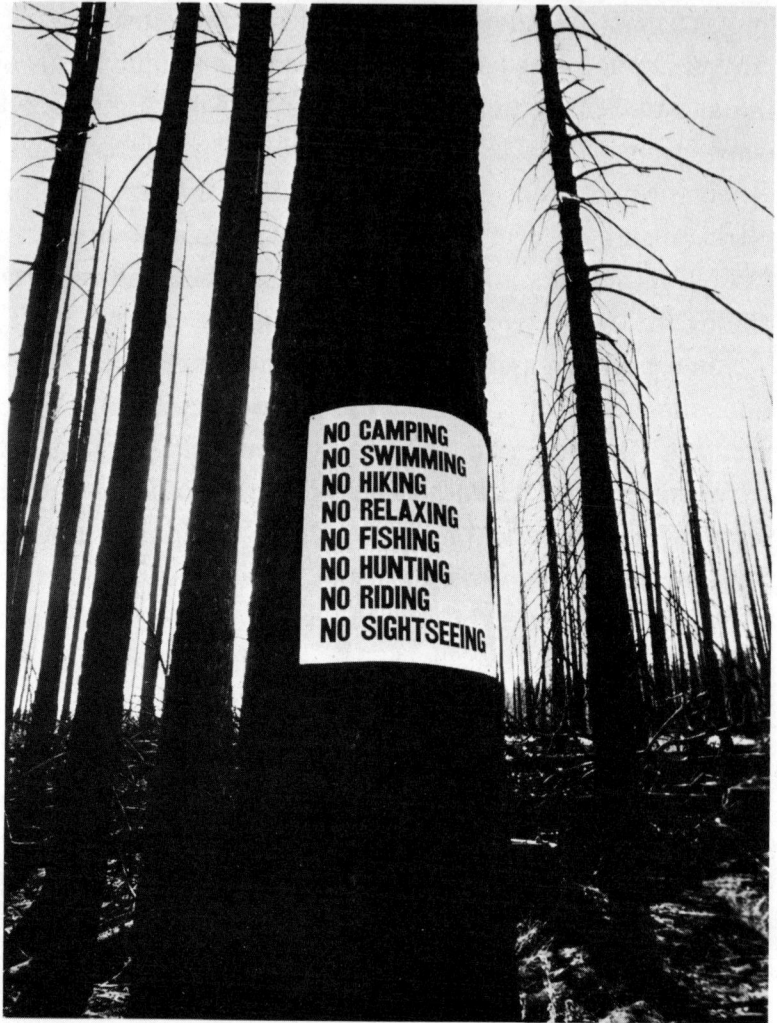

NO CAMPING
NO SWIMMING
NO HIKING
NO RELAXING
NO FISHING
NO HUNTING
NO RIDING
NO SIGHTSEEING

This advertisement to prevent forest fires is a public-service advertisement.

the public about a product or service. Others said advertising was the art of suggestion, or getting people to think and act the way the advertiser wanted. All agreed that advertising was a form of communication. Today, advertising might be defined as the mass distribution of signed and (usually) paid-for messages to influence people to accept a product, service, institution, idea, or point of view. Advertising is most often directed to a great number of people through advertising media such as newspapers or magazines. Media are the means by which the advertising message reaches the consumer — the person who buys the goods and uses the services. The space or time for the advertisement is almost always purchased from the media. Sometimes the media will donate space and time for public-service advertisements, such as Prevent Forest Fires. Advertisers let the public know whom the message is coming from by signing their advertisements.

But advertising is not all big business and mass media. We use it to find apartments, to sell used cars, or to let the community know about a club benefit. In fact, simple messages like these gave advertising its start.

FROM VILLAGE CRIERS TO NETWORK TELEVISION

The history of advertising is the history of advertising media. The first advertising medium was the human voice. Village criers shouted and sang out their advertising messages. In Babylonia, merchants hired barkers to call attention to the goods they had for sale. In Egypt, criers advertised the arrival of ships and their cargoes at the ports of the Nile. Around 3000 B.C. the Babylonians cut the name of a temple and the king who built it in each of the bricks used in the temple's construction. Later, tradesmen and shopowners hung picture-signs over their doors that showed what goods and services were being offered inside. The Rosetta stone, erected in 195 B.C. by the priests of Egypt, "advertised" an Egyptian pharaoh's religious devotion.

The earliest written advertisement that we know about is over three thousand years old. Written on papyrus (a type of paper made from reeds by the ancient Egyptians), it offered a reward for a runaway slave.

The Greeks used public criers to advertise the sale of slaves, animals, and pottery. Criers were selected for their pleasant and convincing voices, as are radio and television announcers today.

Signboards also began to appear in Athens and in Rome. These tablets were hung outside doors and they advertised the name and profession of the occupant. Most signs were pictures because few

A town crier during America's colonial period. (The Bettmann Archive)

people could read. Written advertising became more common as more and more people learned to read and write. Announcements for real estate and circuses were printed in black or red on walls in Pompeii. It is believed that one particular wall was used exclusively for advertising.

During the one thousand years of the Dark Ages, civilization seemed to go backward. Few people could read or write and there

The Rosetta stone.
(Culver Pictures, Inc.)

was little written advertising. However, barkers continued to be popular. Around A.D. 300, merchants at a fair in Britain used barkers to sell their wares. In the twelfth and thirteenth centuries, town criers walked up and down the streets calling out official announcements and legal notices. Later, town criers were permitted to make commercial announcements as well.

It was during the twelfth century that the art of papermaking reached Europe. In the fifteenth century, scribes began to write advertisements. More people were learning to read, so advertisements were tacked up on buildings near where groups of people might gather. All the writing was in Latin and the advertisement usually began: "If anybody desires . . ." or "If anybody knows. . . ." For this reason, they were called *sequis* from the two Latin words *si quis,* which mean "if anybody."

The first advertisement printed in England from movable printing type was a five-by-seven-inch notice for a book. It appeared

William Caxton (center). (The Bettmann Archive)

Advertising in the 1600s. (New York Public
Library Picture Collection)

about 1480, shortly after the invention of printing. It was printed
by William Caxton, who introduced printing to England.

Although signboards continued to be popular in England, printing gave advertising a tremendous boost. At first, laws were an-
nounced by the town crier; but by the seventeenth century printed
handbills and posters had become a more common means for informing the public about new laws. A few years later, leading
English artists and engravers were illustrating handbills and posters
advertising commercial goods.

The first periodicals (similar in appearance to newspapers) were
published in France and England in 1611 and 1612. They pub-

lished public notices similar to the classified advertisements of today. The first real newspaper advertisement in England appeared in 1625 in *The Continuation of Our Weekly Newes*. It was twenty-two years before there was another one, but by the eighteenth century English newspapers were thriving on advertising.

The first advertising in America appeared on the signboards that were hung outside taverns and coffeehouses. Although newspapers were known, the British colonial authorities prevented them from appearing in the colonies for fifty-two years after the first printing press arrived in the New World. In spite of the ban, *Publick Occurences* appeared in 1690. It was promptly suppressed. The third issue of the *Boston News Letter* appeared in 1704 with the first paid advertising in America. Two advertisements offered rewards for lost or stolen merchandise and a third offered some New York real estate for rent.

Two more newspapers appeared in 1719. Benjamin Franklin's brother started a paper in 1721, but Benjamin Franklin took it over in 1728 and renamed it the *Pennsylvania Gazette*. This paper eventually became the magazine called the *Saturday Evening Post*.

Most Americans know that Benjamin Franklin was a great patriot and statesman, but few know that he was also an excellent businessman. He was a printer and publisher, and he did more to develop advertising than anyone else before him. He ran much more advertising than his competitors in the newspaper business. He advertised books, servants, ships' sailings, stationery, tea, lumber, and his own invention, the Franklin stove. Franklin wrote much of the copy (the words) for the advertisements that appeared in

12

Benjamin Franklin wheeling supplies into the office of the *Pennsylvania Gazette*. (The Bettmann Archive)

his paper. He also introduced headlines, small illustrations, new and large type, a new four-page format, and more white space. His ads were much less crowded and much more attractive than those of his competitors.

By the middle of the 1700s, newspapers had grown in size and variety. Previously, all advertisements had been placed at the back of the newspaper; now some appeared toward the front. The first newspaper to become a daily became one (in 1784) largely because it had so much advertising.

Advertising increased after the Civil War. Goods were no longer made in ones and twos at home. Instead, they were being produced in large quantities at factories. It was cheaper to make them this way, but advertising was necessary to help sell all that was produced.

13

A newspaper advertisement for tableware that appeared in 1771 in the New York *Gazette*. (New York Public Library Picture Collection)

The first American magazines appeared in the mid-1880s. They were literary publications with many essays and poems but not many readers. Their publishers resisted advertising in their pages until the need for additional money became great. Slowly, one publisher after another gave in and ran ads. A man named J. Walter Thompson had a great deal to do with convincing publishers to accept advertising, and the advertising agency that bears his name is the largest in the world today.

Also in the 1880s, another man saw great possibilities for magazines. Cyrus H. K. Curtis wanted to produce a magazine that would inform and entertain many people instead of just a select few. He wanted his magazine to have a huge circulation (the circulation of a magazine or newspaper is the number of people who read each issue) and to be profitable, largely because of its advertising. He considered advertising to be a good thing because he believed it would permit him to pay higher prices for quality fiction and art-

14

Cyrus H. K. Curtis. (Culver Pictures, Inc.)

work. This in turn would result in still more readers, more advertising, and more money. Curtis was right. His *Ladies' Home Journal* and *Saturday Evening Post* were among the first magazines to be read by over one million people.

Outdoor advertising in America began with the posting of printed announcements in 1740. By 1780 "billposting," the fastening of advertisements to walls and billboards, was an established occupation. Early billboards used a few short words. Human figures and other artwork were added later to create additional interest.

One of the great users of outdoor advertising at that time was P. T. Barnum. In the 1840s Barnum heavily advertised his American Museum, located on lower Broadway in New York, and his traveling circus, The Greatest Show on Earth. He continually came up with new ideas and challenges for his advertising specialists. One of the biggest ads he ran was a billboard illustration four times

15

Front page of *The Ladies' Home Journal*, 1897. (Culver Pictures, Inc.)

(Culver Pictures, Inc.)

(Culver Pictures, Inc.)

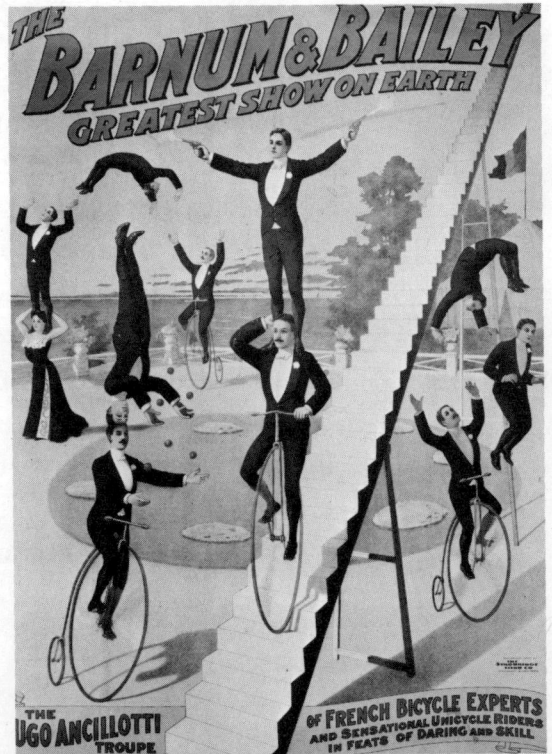

the size of anything that had been printed up to that time. The subject was himself.

Another great outdoor advertiser of the 1860s was John Wanamaker. At the age of twenty-two, Wanamaker started a tremendous clothing store in Philadelphia. He advertised on 100-foot-long signs he had put up along the Pennsylvania Railroad tracks just outside of the city. In one of his advertising campaigns, he sent up hundreds of balloons with advertising messages offering free clothing to anyone who returned a balloon after it floated down.

Radio advertising started in 1922. By 1928 there were five hundred stations, and radio had become a 5-million-dollar business. At first, radio advertising was little more than an announcement of the name of the company and its product. However, the advertising must have produced sales because advertising budgets were large even then. One automobile manufacturer spent half a million dollars on radio advertising in 1928. In the 1930s, radio advertisements (which are called commercials) became longer and included comments on the benefits of the product or service advertised. Sometimes playlets dramatized the use of the product or service.

Radio advertising got a big boost in the mid-1930s when the "soap opera" became popular. The soap opera is a melodrama that features a typical housewife or family who has many personal and family problems to solve. Day after day, for years and years, the shows continued to solve these problems, which never seemed to end. Soap operas were very popular with housewives. Millions listened faithfully for years. Some of the same soap operas are still being followed today on television.

Soap operas got their name because they were most often sponsored (a sponsor is the person, business, or organization that pays the cost of a radio or television program) by soap manufacturers. It was the sponsor's way of reaching the same women day after day to build "brand loyalty." The "brand" is a label or trademark that tells who made the product. While soap operas seem silly to most people, others take them seriously. One sociologist discovered that many women listened to soap operas to get ideas on how to solve their own family problems. This is probably not a good idea because soap operas, like comics, are designed for entertainment, not advice.

About the time that soap operas became popular, advertisers began to look for the most pleasant ways to say the same message over and over again. They decided upon the musical jingle, a simple rhyme set to an easy-to-remember tune. Jingles themselves were not new; they had been popular since the rise of popular music in the 1890s.

Radio reached its peak as an entertainment and advertising medium right after World War II. In 1948 television came along, and the stars, shows, and technicians deserted radio for TV. Seventy percent of radio's audiences went along, and so did the advertisers.

Television was not new. A German scientist built a working television system in 1894, and the French used the term "television" in 1909. Television was demonstrated in 1925 and the first experimental program took place in 1927. Two networks in the United States began broadcasting two to three hours a week in 1939. By 1969, there were 83 million television sets and 847 stations in the country. Television had became the most popular means of mass communication. It has been estimated that over 3 billion

19

dollars was spent on television commercials in America in 1968. In one month, July of 1969, advertisers spent more than 100 million dollars in network television advertising. Television not only reached greater numbers of people; it also let the advertiser demonstrate his product.

TYPES OF ADVERTISING

There are a number of ways to classify advertising. The classifications tell us a great deal about how advertising is planned and used.

Classification by Medium

A *medium* is the means by which advertising and other information is delivered. The plural is *media*. The four major categories of media are print, broadcast, outdoor, and direct mail. Newspapers and magazines, radio and television, are often called *mass media* because they are large public information services. It is natural to categorize advertising by the medium in which it appears, so we have newspaper advertising, magazine advertising, radio and television advertising. The first two are also known as *print* or *space advertising*; the second two are often called *broadcast* or *time advertising*. Broadcast advertisements are called *commercials*. Blank space or time is all the advertiser actually buys from the medium. He arranges for the production of the advertisement himself, and he pays for it separately.

Outdoor advertising includes signs, posters, and billboards on buildings and along the road. (Advertising that appears on buses, subways, and trains is called *transit advertising*.) *Direct-mail ad-*

21

Crowded outdoor advertising along a New Jersey highway. (United Press International)

Transit advertising.

Litter. It's enough to make you sick.
Isn't it enough to make you stop?

Keep America Clean. Keep America Beautiful.

Advertising contributed for the public good.
A public service of Transit Advertising.

vertising uses the United States mail to deliver the advertising brochures, catalogs, order forms, and, ultimately, the ordered merchandise to potential customers. In addition, there are mail-order ads that appear in magazines. The advertised products are ordered and delivered by mail.

Some miscellaneous media include skywriting, the Yellow Pages in the telephone directory, and specialty advertising on ballpoint pens, shopping bags, ashtrays, and other novelties.

Classification by Appearance: Display and Classified Advertising

This classification applies to newspapers and sometimes to magazines. Display ads are the large ads you see throughout the main part of newspapers and magazines. Classified advertisements, or *want ads*, as they are sometimes called, are the smaller advertisements that appear together in the back of the newspaper or magazine.

Display ads are usually sponsored by a company and are meant to sell something to a great many people. They are often illustrated and usually costly. Classified ads are most often placed by individuals and are not very expensive. Usually there is just one item a person wants to sell or buy, or, in the case of employment advertisements, just one job a person wants to have or a company wants to fill.

Classification by Audience: Consumer, Trade, and Industrial Advertising

"Who should see my advertisement?" That is one of the most important decisions an advertiser has to make. It is not always an easy one. He must decide among three main audiences and his choice of one or a combination will depend on what he has to sell and the particular problems he has in selling it. Advertising directed to the general public is called *consumer advertising*. Advertising directed to the owners and managers of the stores that sell his product (to the consumer) is called *trade advertising*. Advertising to other businesses that will use his product or service to make its own product or service is called *industrial advertising*.

Classification by What Is Advertised

There is advertising for airlines, automobiles, clothing, television repairmen, laundries, charities, colleges, and political candidates. Each of these can be considered as a type of advertising in itself. Or we can say that advertising for items such as automobiles, clothing, and food can all be thought of as *product advertising*. Airlines, television repairmen, and window cleaners all advertise services, so their advertising can be thought of as *service advertising*.

Other types of advertising do not attempt to sell a company's products or services, but are aimed instead at gaining acceptance of the company itself or of an idea the company favors. This is called *institutional advertising*. In a 1969 issue of *Time* magazine,

24

Product advertising. (Doyle, Dane, Bernbach, Inc., for Galey & Lord)

SOD
5¢

Galey&Lord

Permanent-press two-ply yarn-dyed polyester/cotton knit by Galey & Lord—
a division of Burlington Industries at Burlington House, New York, N.Y. 10019.

for example, the Anaconda Company advertised the economic usefulness of its mining activities, and the Martin Marietta Company advertised the many activities (from cement to spacecraft) of its group of smaller associated companies. Advertisements that promote some generally accepted value such as supporting our schools or preventing forest fires are called *public service* advertisements. There are many more categories: employment advertising, educational advertising (for a particular college, for example), and political advertising, to name just a few.

Classification by Type of Advertiser: Manufacturer or Dealer

Manufacturers make products. Dealers buy them in quantity and sell them to the public. They are usually separate companies. Manufacturers such as the Ford Motor Company or General Mills usually do a substantial amount of the more expensive magazine and television advertising. But local dealers or retail merchants, who actually sell the item directly to the consumer, often advertise a great deal too. Sometimes a manufacturer will give the dealer a certain amount of money to advertise the manufacturer's product, or he will match the amount the dealer spends. This is called *cooperative advertising*.

Classification by Area: National, Regional, and Local Advertising

If a company's products or services are available throughout all or most of the country, the company will usually use *national advertising*. Automobiles, cereals, soaps, soft drinks, and refrigerators are some of the many products advertised in national magazines and over national chains of radio and television stations called *networks*. National advertising accounts for about two thirds of all advertising in America.

Most *local advertising* is done by local businesses and retail stores who want to reach only the people living in their business area. Department stores, automobile dealers, photography stores, record stores, and neighborhood banks are some of the many local businesses that advertise in daily and weekly newspapers and over

26

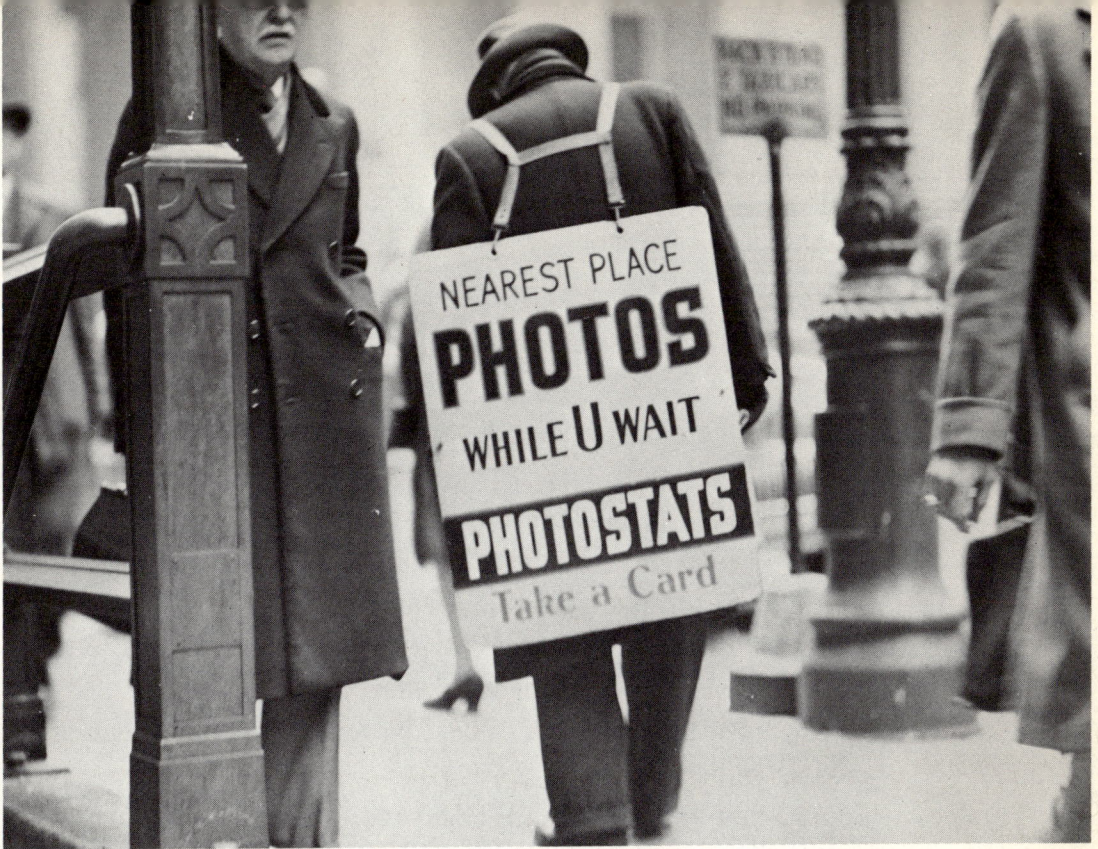

Local advertising in New York City. (The Bettmann Archive)

local radio and (sometimes) television stations. Local advertising accounts for about one third of all advertising in America.

Advertising that falls somewhere between national and local is called *regional* or *sectional advertising*. This advertising may appear in just part of a state or may be placed in one or more sections of the country, such as the Midwest or the South.

There are still more ways of classifying advertising, but these are some of the more important ones.

MODERN MEDIA

Choosing the media is one of the advertiser's most important decisions.

Newspapers reach large groups of people, are fairly inexpensive, and allow the advertiser to pinpoint his audience geographically. They are more flexible than other types of media because they are put together every twenty-four hours (or weekly), and ads can be scheduled and changed on short notice.

The advertiser must consider, however, that reproduction of pictures in newspapers is not as good as in magazines. Newspapers do not show as much detail. Color reproduction, where available, is also not as good except for color ads that are printed on special, better-grade paper and inserted into the newspaper. These *preprints* are very expensive, however.

Newspaper space is sold by the *agate line*. An agate line is one column wide by one-fourteenth of an inch deep. One reason that the agate line is used as a standard newspaper measure is that the column width varies among newspapers. When an advertiser wants to run an ad, he specifies the amount of space he wants (the number of agate lines) and the dimensions of the ad (number of columns wide and number of inches deep). Let us say an advertiser wants to run a five hundred (agate) line ad. He can choose to run the ad two columns wide and about eighteen inches deep, four columns

Maybe you need glasses?

Or gas.
At Mobil, we'll take care of both at once.
Drive into a participating Mobil dealer station. And pick up one of these attractive glasses.
Take your choice: 9 or 12 ounce size. All in festive amber-colored dot pattern.
Show us no mercy. Stop in a hundred times, and get enough glasses for a block party.
You can get Mobil's great Detergent Gasoline, too. And you don't need glasses to see how terrific that is.

Mobil.

Free with any purchase
at participating Mobil dealer.

A 600-line black-and-white newspaper advertisement. (Doyle, Dane, Bernbach, Inc., for Mobil Oil Corp.)

wide and about nine inches deep, or some other combination of columns wide and inches deep.

Many national advertisers use newspapers, but newspaper advertising is most popular with local businesses. It makes good advertising sense for a neighborhood clothing store, dry cleaner, or gasoline station to advertise its special sales only to its local market. In newspaper advertising in 1968, local advertisers spent 4 billion dollars — more than four times as much as national advertisers.

The costs of newspaper ads vary according to the circulation of the paper and the size of the ad. In 1969, the New York *Daily News,* with a circulation of over two million, charged $4,740 for a page of advertising. In the same year, the Detroit *Free Press,* with a circulation of 600,803, charged $3,840 per page, and the St. Louis *Post Dispatch,* with a circulation of 387,180, charged $2,976.

Magazines are the other major print medium. There are two main types of magazines: consumer (numbering approximately 650) and business, trade, and technical (numbering approximately 2,350). Consumer magazines are also classified as "mass" or "class" magazines. Mass magazines are "family" magazines and have large circulations. Circulation figures include both newsstand sales and subscriptions, copies people receive by mail after paying a yearly rate. *Life* and *Look* are two well-known examples of mass magazines. So is the *Reader's Digest*, which goes to approximately 17 million people each month.

Class magazines are special-interest publications that appeal to certain well-defined consumer groups. *Modern Photography* is of special interest to camera fans. *Popular Mechanics* is for the man who likes to build things. *Boys' Life, American Girl,* and *Jack and Jill* appeal to young people.

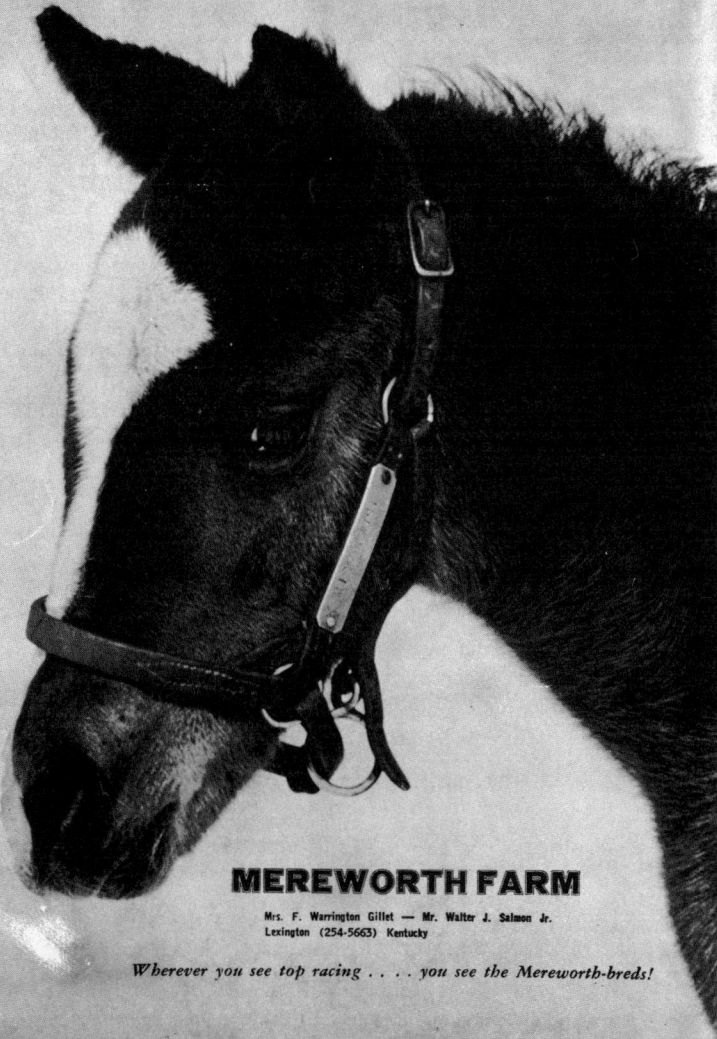

OUR FIRST 1970 FOAL

MEREWORTH FARM

Mrs. F. Warrington Gillet — Mr. Walter J. Salmon Jr.
Lexington (254-5663) Kentucky

Wherever you see top racing . . . . you see the Mereworth-breds!

Bay colt by T.V. Lark -- Miss Twist, by Prince John

An advertisement for Mereworth Farm, a large Thoroughbred-horse breeding farm in Kentucky. This advertisement was placed on the back cover of *The Bloodhorse,* a class magazine sent weekly by subscription to owners, breeders, trainers, and those people interested in racing.

Magazines have many advantages for advertisers. They reach great numbers of people and are often seen more than once by the same person. Unlike newspapers, magazines are usually kept around the house or office for up to a week or month or more. Mass magazines reach many different kinds of people. The quality of magazine printing is superb, and pictures are shown in very good detail. Color is almost always available if the advertiser is willing to pay the extra charge. Products that appeal to the eye, such as fabrics and food, are especially good for magazine advertising.

Many advertising professionals believe that the magazine's *image* often rubs off on the products advertised in its pages. The image is the total impression made by the magazine on the public. How do people feel about the magazine? Do they look upon it as old or young? Modern or traditional? Drab or colorful? *Vogue* has a sophisticated, feminine, high-fashion image. *Popular Mechanics* has a practical, masculine, no-nonsense image. Advertisers try to choose magazines with the right image for their product.

Magazine advertising costs are based on circulation and the size of the ad. Space is sold by the page and in fractions of a page, and the full-page ad is the most commonly desired. A full-page black-and-white ad might cost anywhere from about $200 for a trade magazine going to a few hundred wholesale candy merchants up to $42,400 for *Life* magazine going to over 8½ million people. Color ads are more expensive; for example, a four-color, full-page ad in *Life* in 1969 cost $64,200.

If the advertiser wants to advertise on the inside front or inside back cover of a magazine — pages that receive more reader attention — he must pay more than the inside page rate. The outside back cover of the same magazine costs the advertiser still more. An advertiser might also want to make a big splash with a *two-page spread,* two facing pages inside the magazine — at double the one-page cost, of course. A *bleed* ad also costs more. "Bleed" is a term for an illustration that runs into the margin of a page.

In 1969, the Radio Advertising Bureau estimated that there were 282 million radio sets in America. Although most of these sets are in homes, 79 million are in cars and public places. People listen to the radio while driving to and from work, while sitting on a beach, or while working in the house or garage. In spite of television, people still do a lot of radio listening. Advertisers deserted radio when television became popular, but they are once again beginning to see the advantages of advertising on radio.

People listen to the radio almost everywhere. (United Press International)

Television made radio a local medium like newspapers. There are still a few network shows that are heard coast to coast on radio, but most shows are local. A few local stations broadcast nothing but news twenty-four hours a day. Most, however, concentrate on music and mix it with news, weather, public-service announcements, and commercials.

Besides taking away many of radio's major attractions, television also changed radio's *prime time.* Prime time is the time during which the station has the greatest number of listeners. For this reason, many radio and television advertisers want their commercials aired during this time even though it costs more. In the 1930s and 1940s, prime-time radio used to be from about 7:00 P.M. to 10:00 P.M. — after dinner, when the family relaxed by sitting around and listening to the radio. Today it is between 6:00 A.M. and 9:00 A.M. and 4:00 P.M. and 7:00 P.M. That is when people are going to and coming from work — too busy to watch television but often listening to radios at the breakfast table and in their cars.

Local advertisers who do not have the money to spend on television advertising often use radio to good advantage. Sound-oriented commercials are most effective. One recent award-winning minute commercial featured nothing but a ringing telephone and a man running, running, running and panting, panting, panting up a seemingly endless flight of stairs. This went on for a full forty-five seconds until at last he picked up the phone, and still panting heavily, said hello. All he heard was a dial tone — the caller had hung up. The words that followed were simplicity itself, something like: "Wouldn't it be easier to get an extension telephone? Call your telephone business office." It made the point. Television pictures could not have improved that commercial.

34

Watching television while enjoying noonday refreshments in Rome, Italy. (United Press International)

The basic advertising unit in radio — at least the most common one — is the one-minute commercial. Other common *time buys* are the twenty- and thirty-second commercials. Still another is the *ten-second I.D.*, or *identification,* commercial, just enough time for a *name and claim,* an identification of the product and a brief statement of its major benefit.

In the late 1960s, a one-minute commercial on a radio network cost about $800 to $1,500. The same time over a single, popular, large-city radio station would cost the advertiser about $100. The

35

cost of broadcast time does not include production costs for the sounds that go into it. The exception to this is a simple script read by the station's own announcer.

Television is more than sound and pictures. Television is sound and pictures and *movement*. Movement is probably television's greatest advantage to advertisers. Television attracts huge audiences, but so does radio. Television uses music and sound effects, but radio does that also. Television can show people and products, but so can the print media — often in true color and better detail. However, only television can offer all of these things together and show movement as well. Movement is more than an interesting technique or gimmick. It permits the advertiser to demonstrate his product and what it does. The demonstration may be as obvious as comparing two kitchen cleansers side by side in the sink, or it may be as subtle as a smile after a man tastes a soft drink. Many advertising people believe that television is the most exciting medium and the most effective too. In 1968 advertisers spent over 3 billion dollars a year for television time on 665 commercial television stations. Only one sixth of this money was spent by local advertisers; national advertisers spent the rest.

In the early days of television, it was common for a single advertiser to sponsor a nationally televised weekly show. To sponsor a show meant that the advertiser not only paid for the three commercial minutes in a half-hour show, but he paid for the production of the show itself. This assured his continued association with the show, and it could be quite an advantage if the show became popular. Some examples are the Kraft Music Hall, a musical variety show sponsored by the Kraft Foods Division of the National Dairy

36

The Bell Telephone Hour was a nationally televised show that ran twice a month. (NBC Photo)

Products Corp., the G.E. College Bowl, a quiz show featuring two teams of college students and sponsored by the General Electric Company, and the Union Carbide Corporation's 21st Century, a program showing how we are likely to be living in the next century.

Television advertising is expensive. One minute of prime-time network television costs from about forty to fifty thousand dollars. A very popular event like a football game, a World Series game, or an entertainment special can cost the advertiser as much as a hundred thousand dollars a minute. As television production and commercial time costs increased, single sponsorships became rare. Today it is more common for several advertisers to sponsor a show together as *participating sponsors*.

Another way around the high cost of television commercials is the television *spot*. Spot commercials are not tied to a national network show. They run in certain general time periods during the day or week, but the exact time at which they appear is up to the station. If the time is available, a spot advertiser can buy time on as many or as few stations as he wants. He can run a greater number of commercials at the time he is having a new introduction or a special sale.

The length of the commercial is not all that determines how much the time will cost. Also important is the time of day during which it will be telecast. Prime-time television runs from 7:30 P.M. to 11:00 P.M. It is the most popular viewing time and the most expensive for advertisers. *Early fringe* is from 5:00 P.M. to 7:30 P.M., about the same as prime-time radio. *Late fringe* is from 11:00 P.M. to when the station signs off the air, and *daytime* is from the time the station begins telecasting in the morning until 5:00 P.M.

Sometimes an advertiser will buy a minute of commercial time but put two thirty-second commercials for different products in it. This is called *piggybacking*. Although stations do limit the number of minutes allotted to commercials in an hour, this piggybacking, plus station announcements, opening and closing program announcements, public-service announcements, and more, can make the time between program changes quite hectic. Viewers and even

38

advertisers get annoyed, and advertising and television people are continually discussing ways this clutter can be reduced. Their discussions have not been very helpful. TV commercial clutter remains a problem.

Media are very careful to avoid placing competing advertisements next to each other. If this occurs or if some technical difficulty prevents good reproduction or delivery of the commercial, the advertiser or agency may ask for a *make-good*. This is another showing at no extra charge. With television time going for about fifty thousand dollars a minute, any mistake can be very costly to the station or network.

In the early days of television there were many live shows and commercials. Both are disappearing. Too often, embarrassing mistakes occurred. There were scores of catastrophes like the easy-to-open refrigerator door that would not open, the quick-light lighter that would not light at all, and the lady who got her dress caught in the car door she was closing. As funny as these mistakes were to the television audience, pity the poor advertiser who was paying all that money to make his product look good. Today most major advertisers have their commercials produced on film or on video tape so there will be no mistakes.

Outdoor advertising, better known as *billboards*, is as common as television and just as controversial. Two thousand national advertisers spent over 225 million dollars on over a quarter of a million billboards in 1968. This figure does not include the thousands of local signs and posters that you see along the road for motels, restaurants, shopping centers, and places of entertainment.

Although billboards are colorful, they cannot talk, are stationary, and almost never have more than four to six words. Why do advertisers use them? Because they are good for two important jobs — introducing a new product and reminding people to buy an old one. These messages from gasoline, food, airline, and other companies are placed where they can be seen easily and read quickly by tens of thousands of passing motorists and pedestrians.

Outdoor advertising has been attacked by many Americans be-

In the early days of television there were many live commercials. Today, most commercials are filmed. Here, a camera crew films a commercial for an automobile company. (Doyle, Dane, Bernbach, Inc.)

Billboards almost never contain more than four to six words in their advertisements. These billboards were put up near Harrisburg, Pennsylvania, in spite of the state's anti-billboard laws. (United Press International)

This billboard in Jefferson Township, New Jersey, was put up by an unknown citizen. It very effectively slowed motorists near a dangerous curve on the highway. (United Press International)

cause it detracts from the scenic beauty of the countryside. Many of these billboards are put on privately owned land and represent additional income for the owners. Because of this it is often hard to control the quantity of these signs. Yet the effect of too many billboards on scenery is of growing concern, and many attempts are being made to limit their use.

Billboards are made up of printed sheets that are pasted side by side. The overall size of the standard panel on which they are pasted is 12 x 25 feet. The size of the picture area inside varies. Billboard space is bought by the month and usually costs from fifty to seventy-five dollars per billboard. Sometimes special *painted bulletins* are put up. These are single posters for heavy-traffic areas, and the space is usually bought by the year. They are considerably larger than the standard panel, sometimes as large as 12 x 48 feet or 12 x 60 feet. They are so expertly painted that you cannot tell them from printed posters.

Direct mail — the advertising that reaches you through the mail — is probably the most misunderstood advertising medium. Those advertising leaflets, brochures, and catalogs that you and your family pull from your mailbox are the most scientifically designed advertisements in the world. Yet they are often called junk mail and tossed in the wastebasket. However, people do read some of these leaflets and brochures and are influenced by them. Like any other kind of advertising, direct mail works or advertisers simply would not use it.

Direct mail is very popular with advertisers. Over 275,000 organizations hold the special mailing permit used for most direct mail. Direct-mail advertisers give the post office so much business that they get a special discount on quantity mailings. It is called a *bulk rate,* and without it, direct-mail advertising would be too expensive. The bulk-rate mailings are not delivered as fast as regular first-class (letter) mail, and that is one of the reasons it costs less per piece.

Because you and your family throw away so much direct-mail advertising — sometimes without even opening it — it may seem strange to you that so much is sent out. Direct-mail advertisers seldom expect to get more than a few orders for every hundred mailing pieces they send. In many cases advertisers may only need orders

43

The postman delivers direct-mail advertising. (United Press International)

from 4 to 5 percent of the people to whom they send the mailing piece to make a profit.

The real advantage of direct mail is that advertisers can pinpoint the people most likely to respond to their advertising. Direct-mail advertisers have more control over audience selection. They rent mailing lists from firms that collect lists of names and addresses of people with special characteristics, such as a certain age, income, location of residence, sex, past buying habits, or special interests.

Other mailing lists feature groups such as car owners, brides, sailing-club members, and new home buyers. Some homes get more than one of the same mailing piece because they are on more than one mailing list. It is cheaper for the advertiser to send you a second mailing piece than to check over the tens of thousands of names for those people who may be on both lists.

It is very hard to talk about direct-mail costs. There is no standard unit in direct mail as there is for a page in a magazine or a minute of broadcast time. The printing costs of direct-mail advertising vary considerably — the larger the number of pieces printed the less the cost per piece to the advertiser. The amount of color in the mailing, the size and shape of the envelope, the number of pieces put into the envelope (many mailings may include a color brochure, an introductory letter, an order form, and a return envelope) all determine the cost to the advertiser.

THE ADVERTISING AGENCY

Many different kinds of organizations use advertising — manu-facturers, service companies, colleges, charities, and political groups. Many of these organizations do their own advertising, especially if their advertising budgets are small. Larger organiza-tions, or those that do a great deal of advertising, hire business firms called advertising agencies to help them create, produce, schedule, and test their advertising campaigns. They become the advertising agency's customer, or *client*. The agency may work with the com-pany's advertising manager or an entire group of men who make up a large advertising or marketing department.

However, advertising agencies did not always work for advertis-ers. The growth of the advertising agency parallels the growth of newspaper advertising. At first, the newspaper itself sold advertis-ing space. The first advertising agents were the colonial postmasters who were authorized to accept and forward advertisements to pub-lications. (Most newspaper publishers, with the exception of a few like Benjamin Franklin, did not want to get involved with adver-tising at all.) Then space brokers appeared. They would buy all the advertising space in one or more newspapers and resell it to advertisers at a profit.

In the 1840s, two advertising agencies were formed: John L. Hooper had an office in New York and Volney B. Palmer had

46

The Peace Corps is only one of many organizations that uses advertising.

offices in Boston, New York, and Philadelphia. Their agencies just sold space and made sure the advertisement appeared as ordered. They would look after production details such as typesetting and platemaking, but they did not do any writing or artwork for their clients.

In the 1890s advertising agencies found it was easier to sell a potential advertiser a selling idea than it was to sell them a blank page in a newspaper. So the agency began to help the advertiser in the writing of the advertising copy and the design of the trademark and artwork.

About this time, the advertising agencies began to switch their allegiance from the newspapers, whose space they sold, to the advertisers, for whom they did creative work. But many agencies today still get their income as if they worked for the media; they

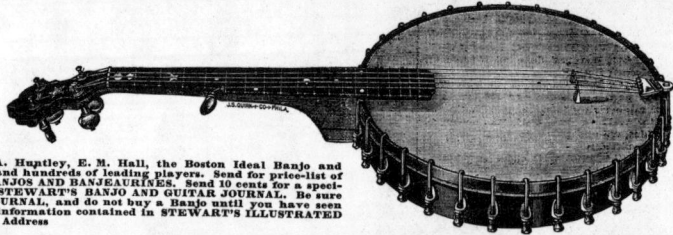

In the 1890s the advertising agency began to help advertisers write the copy for advertisements such as these. (New York Public Library Picture Collection)

receive a commission from the media on the space and time sold to the advertiser. The media bill the advertising agency for the amount of time or space bought by the advertising agency's client, less 15 percent. The agency in turn bills its client for the full cost of the time and space, keeping the 15 percent for wages, rent, and other expenses. For large agencies, about 1½ percent can be called profit.

The original advertising agencies were usually one-man operations. As agencies grew larger they found that some people excelled in creating the advertising words and pictures while others were best at developing plans and schedules and selling time to a client. Thus began the basic division of labor found in many advertising agencies today.

The Account Executive

A client or his advertising business is known as the *account*. There is usually one account executive for each account, although very large accounts may have two or more executives who handle different parts of the client's advertising program.

Account executives work differently in different advertising agencies, but almost all are responsible for keeping in contact with the client and helping him to plan the entire campaign. This means that the account executive must know everything possible about the advertiser's business and product. He must know how the product is made, distributed, and sold, what the advertiser's competition is, and what the competition's advertising and selling plans are. He

The creative director (right of board) and the account executive (left) at a planning session. (Doyle, Dane, Bernbach, Inc.)

must discuss with his client how much to spend on the advertising campaign and the best way to spend it.

An example of decisions the account executive and client work out together is whether to use a *pull* or a *push* strategy. A pull strategy aims at getting consumers to ask for the product by brand name so the store will stock it. Consumer advertising is the key tool in this strategy. A push strategy relies on getting the manufacturer's, wholesaler's, and retailer's selling force to push the brand down the marketing channels to the ultimate consumer. Agency and client must also decide if the ads should be run nationally by the manufacturer, or locally by dealers who sell his product, or both. They must decide if the campaign should increase *primary* or *secondary demand*. Primary-demand ads promote a product as a whole, rather than a particular brand. The American Dairy Association, for example, promotes the drinking of milk in general. Secondary-demand ads stress a specific brand of a product, such as Borden's milk. The advertiser may choose a primary-demand campaign if he has a product so new or so different that there is not really much competition. Another reason he may choose a primary-demand campaign is if he has so much of the business that he can afford to let his competitors benefit from a small increase in sales from his advertising.

The account executive also helps his client decide if he wants a *direct-action* or *indirect-action campaign*. Direct-action ads ask the reader or listener to order right away, either by using a coupon on the ad or by telephoning a number given on radio or television. But most advertising is indirect, and any one ad merely contributes to the total effort that leads the consumer to buy. It is difficult to imagine anyone ordering a soft drink or a new car by mail.

The account executive also collects materials from supervisors in the copy, art, media, research, and merchandising departments of the agency to make a *presentation* of the agency's campaign recommendations to the client. One of the best descriptions of a good account executive is that he must be the best at selling the client the campaign and second best at everything else. Once the client approves the overall plan, the account executive works with the other departments which create, produce, and schedule the specific ads and commercials.

51

Copywriters

The copywriter is the man or woman who must come up with "the big idea." This is usually the campaign theme or slogan — the key phrase that will hopefully solve in a few words all the problems discussed in pages of research reports. The copywriter often tries the product himself. He talks to many people about it, reads research reports, and may even visit the client's factory to see how the product is made. What the copywriter must do is sum up the product's major benefit in a dramatic, convincing, attention-getting way. Once he has an idea, he writes a headline and body copy, or text, to explain the idea further. When writing radio and television commercials, the copywriter also suggests music, sound effects, and pictures where they are appropriate.

Art Directors

Even though the copywriter is the man responsible for the big idea, he is often given more credit for it than he deserves. The print or television art director is almost always in on the creation of the idea right from the beginning. In fact, good art directors are idea men first and artists second.

Print art directors almost never do the finished art for newspaper and magazine ads. Their rough sketches are often scribbly, scratchy lines and big blobs of color. Picture ideas are what they get paid for.

In the first stages of creating an idea, the print art director works very fast and that is why his sketches are so rough. He does many of

52

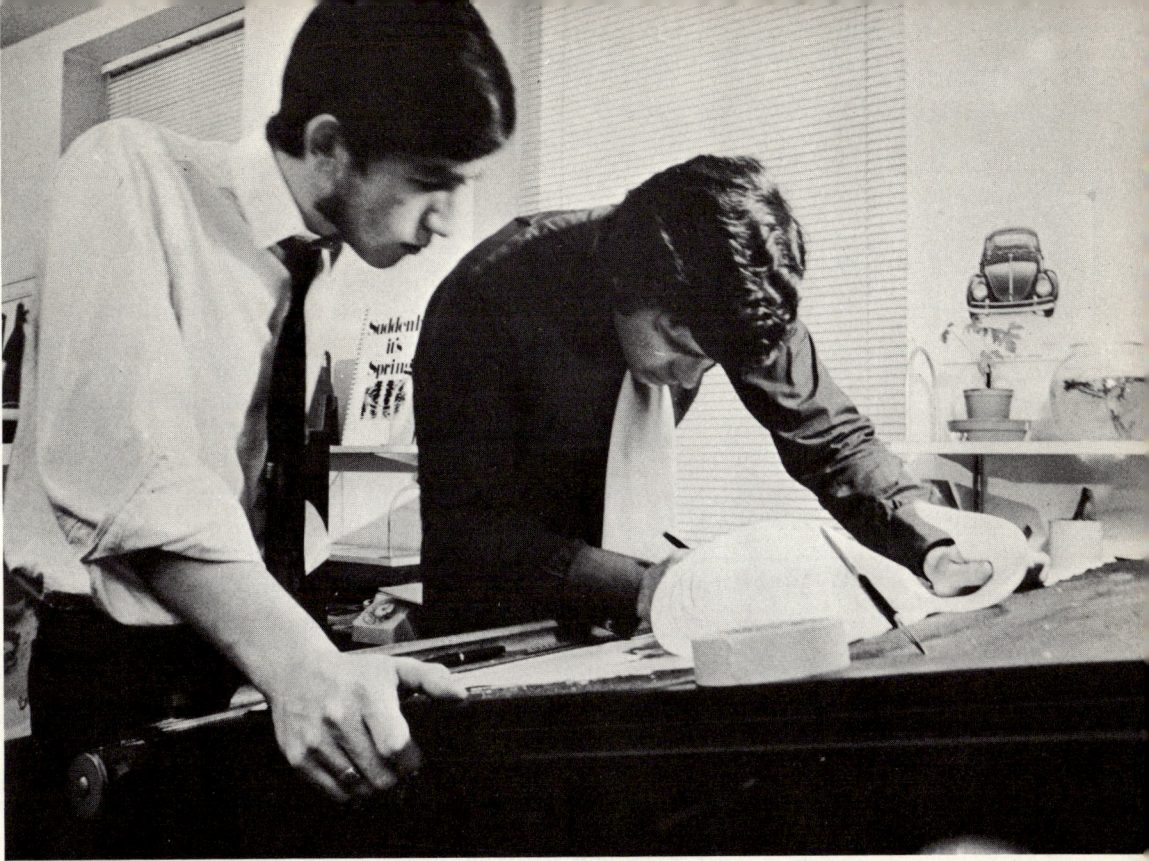

Working on the roughs for an advertisement. (Doyle, Dane, Bernbach, Inc.)

them and relies heavily on his copywriter's ability to visualize the idea — to imagine it. If the print art director's roughs are small and sketchy, they are called *thumbnail roughs* or *thumbnails.* If they are larger but still barely recognizable in outline form (maybe with a little shading or color), they are just called *roughs,* and if they are pretty good drawings or sketches of what the final picture will look like, they may qualify as a *comprehensive.* A comprehensive layout almost always includes the copywriter's headline, accu-

53

rately lettered to show the kind of printing type, an indication of where the text is to go, and the space for the advertiser's signature. The client is often shown a comprehensive to get a good idea of how the finished ad will look.

Once the comprehensive layout is approved, the print art director is responsible for artistic supervision during its production. He must know enough about the technical processes of reproduction — printing, engraving, lithography, typography, and photography — to discuss problems with the production manager. He will also hire and supervise the illustrators and photographers, who are independent businessmen and operate outside the agency.

The television art director must also be an idea man. Instead of doing layouts, he does a *storyboard*, a series of a half-dozen to twenty or so small sketches of what is to appear on the television screen. These sketches guide the film or video-tape production people who actually make the commercial.

The Agency TV and Film Producer

The agency TV and film producer must see that the words and pictures on the television storyboard get turned into sounds and film or video tape. He must check the pace of the commercial to see if it is appropriately fast and lively or slow and moody. He selects the right music and sound effects and picks the actors, director, and production (sound, film, or TV) studio. If it is a television commercial, he also coordinates the activities of the studio's set designer and the wardrobe (costume) and makeup people. He is also

54

An audio control room and sound studio. Sound is frequently added after the scenes are filmed. In this studio, actors or announcers can watch the commercial on the screen and synchronize their voices with the action. (Reeves Production Services)

in charge of production costs. It often takes a full eight-hour day or more to produce a sixty-second commercial. Studios can cost six hundred dollars an hour and commercials can cost ten to twenty thousand dollars just to produce.

55

Creative Supervision

Up until the early 1960s, copywriters, art directors, and producers were all in separate departments in the advertising agency. Today it is more common to find them all together in a *creative group* (or team) along with copy and art supervisors and an overall creative supervisor or creative group head. Each creative group is assigned to one or more accounts. The agency's creative director supervises all the groups.

The Media Man

Media people are numbers people. Their principal job is to pick the right number and types of media to reach the maximum number of the right kind of audience for a particular advertisement. The media person must match the media to the market he is trying to reach and sell. One of his basic decisions in choosing among media is whether to buy *reach* (the largest possible number of people) or *frequency* (reaching fewer people more times). That means he will have to decide between advertising once or twice in a few large national magazines, or many times in many local newspapers. The media person must also know the editorial content, format, and image of the media. He must know their special features, discounts, and special opportunities, such as foldout pages.

56

MARY HAD AN ASHTRAY

by HENRY GIBSON

Mary had an ashtray
Full of ashes white as snow
And every time she drove her car
The tray would overflow.
She dumped it on the road one day
Which was against the rule.
The road is very ugly now
'Cause she was such a fool.

Keep America Clean.
Keep America Beautiful.

The media man picks the right media for the message. (Lennen & Newell, Inc., advertising contributed for the public good)

The Merchandising Department

Most advertising agencies help their client with more than advertising alone. They may also work in other areas of the client's marketing operation. Marketing is *all* the tools an organization uses to sell its products or services — advertising, salesmen, public relations, sales promotion, merchandising, and research. The marketing *mix* is the combination of all these methods of selling. The merchandising department may help the client design logotypes (symbols that represent the company) and packaging. How a package is shaped, how a label reads, the material the package is made out of — all are worked on in the merchandising department. One shampoo advertiser set its entire advertising campaign around the fact that its product came in a nonbreakable container, easy

Counter-display advertising.

and safe to carry into the shower with you. The merchandising department also works on *counter display* or *point-of-purchase* advertisements. These are the small advertisements that stand near counters and cash registers.

The Research Department

Advertising research people sometimes have backgrounds in marketing, but often it is in other fields such as psychology, sociology, or statistics. Psychologists and sociologists search for the reasons why consumers behave as they do. Statisticians and others try to find out how many people act in these different ways. Research tries to find out who might use the product or service, where these consumers are, what they are like, what they read, listen to, or look at, how well they like or remember the ads, and how effective the advertising was in getting them to buy the product or use the service.

59

RESEARCH

Many advertising campaigns are based on the results of research. There are many kinds of research and they often overlap.

Market research, sometimes called consumer research, is concerned with who buys the product, who uses it, why and how it is used, how much is bought and used at one time, how often it is bought and where, habits which affect its use, consumer attitudes toward the product and the company, shopping habits, and how "loyal" the consumer is to the brand. Researchers gather many facts about the consumer, such as age, sex, income, family size, and occupation. These are called *demographic* characteristics. Some are determined when a client introduces a new product in a *test* market, a small selection of cities or areas used to test consumer response to the product and its advertising. From market research we have learned that people on the east and west coasts of the United States like mayonnaise, while people in the central regions of the nation prefer whipped salad dressing. We have also learned that it is easier to sell an electric razor to a man who already has one than to a man who has never bought one.

Media research deals with how many and what kind of people read certain magazines and newspapers, watch certain television programs, and listen to certain radio shows. Media researchers can obtain highly accurate readership information about the number

The A. C. Nielsen Company's Instantaneous Audimeter, an electronic recording device that can be attached to a TV set.

of issues of newspapers and magazines sold. The Audit Bureau of Circulation is the principal organization that specializes in gathering circulation data for media people. The print media themselves often issue circulation and reader research studies.

Unlike the print media, most radio and television audience research is done by independent research companies such as the A. C. Nielsen Co. These companies try to find out about audience size, the type of people who listen to different radio and television shows, and their attitudes and ideas. Several different methods are used. Interviewers go house to house and ask people what television or radio programs and commercials they saw or heard that day. Another research method is called *telephone-coincidental*. Here, researchers make many telephone calls to homes "coincident" with the program; that is, while it is on the air. If the person is watching or listening, the researcher asks him questions on the spot. Still another approach, the *diary approach*, gets a group of typical listeners or viewers to keep a diary or written record of what programs they watch or listen to. Electronic recording devices attached to the radio or television set are the most accurate means of finding out when the set is in use and what station or channel it was turned to at a particular time. But even these devices cannot guarantee that anyone was actually in the room while the set was turned on.

Advertising research attempts to measure advertising effectiveness. *Pretests* helps the advertiser decide what to say in advertising and how to say it. *Post-tests* try to determine how well the advertisement performed after it ran.

Opinion ratings are one type of pretest. In opinion ratings, researchers ask individual consumers or a panel of consumers which of two or more ads they think is best and why. Consumers may rate a print ad on such points as headline, picture, text, believability, ease of understanding, attractiveness, and so on. To pretest television commercials, the agency shows the panel a *filmograph*, a motion picture film of the storyboard sketches or still photographs of the commercial.

Split-run inquiry tests are another way of pretesting print advertisements. Two versions of an ad can be prepared and each run in half of the newspapers or magazines. Both versions ask the reader to send for more information or to order what is advertised. Each version has a *code* number on its coupon to indicate to the advertiser which ad it is from. This code may be a series of numbers or

Nielsen's Instantaneous Audimeter system, which computes ratings from electronic recordings of TV-set usage and transmits them to a client's office.

letters at the bottom of the coupon, or it may be a department number in the address. The advertiser simply adds up the number of coupons with each different code number and sees which advertisement pulled the most responses. This can be considered a pretest only if a large number of ads will be placed later as a result of the test.

A common post-test is the *recognition test*. In this test an interviewer shows the consumer a copy of a magazine or newspaper, page by page, to find out which ads the consumer recognizes. Some advertising people believe that recognition tests are not accurate enough, so they ask that *aided recall* tests be given. In an aided recall test, the interviewer gives the consumer a list of brand names, some of which appeared in the magazine or newspaper he read, some of which did not. The consumer is asked to identify the ads he saw by brand name and tell about the ad: what it said, what it looked like, what the sales points were. *Pure recall* tests require that the consumer tell the interviewer what ads he saw and what he remembered about them without any aids at all.

In the late 1950s and early 1960s, motivation research attracted a great deal of public attention. Researchers discovered that the reasons people gave for buying one product rather than another were often not the real reasons. Instead, people were prompted to act by unconscious motives, those they could not or would not admit even to themselves. Motivation researchers believe that these motives play a larger role in a consumer's purchase of a product than the customer's expressed reasons.

How do motivation researchers find these hidden or forgotten reasons? One way is to give *projective* tests. For example, you ask

64

Lemon.

This Volkswagen missed the boot.

The chrome strip on the glove compartment is blemished and must be replaced. Chances are you wouldn't have noticed it; Inspector Kurt Kroner did.

There are 3,389 men at our Wolfsburg factory with only one job: to inspect Volkswagens at each stage of production. (3000 Volkswagens are produced daily; there are more inspectors than cars.)

Every shock absorber is tested (spot checking won't do), every windshield is scanned. VWs have been rejected for surface scratches barely visible to the eye.

Final inspection is really something! VW inspectors run each car off the line onto the Funktionsprüfstand (car test stand), tote up 189 check points, gun ahead to the automatic brake stand, and say "no" to one VW out of fifty.

This preoccupation with detail means the VW lasts longer and requires less maintenance, by and large, than other cars. (It also means a used VW depreciates less than any other car.)

We pluck the lemons; you get the plums.

The car in this advertisement is so well known because of advertising that the agency can label it "Lemon" and still have the consumer recall the brand name. (Doyle, Dane, Bernbach, Inc., for Volkswagen of America, Inc.)

someone to complete a sentence like: "People who buy Adams ice cream are _____." The person answering the question will invent an answer. What he invents will tell something about how *he* feels about Adams ice cream.

There are other kinds of projective tests. Another way of finding out what people really think about themselves or a product is to give two groups of people a list of words describing someone, let us say a housewife. Both groups get the same list with one exception. One group's housewife uses brand X, the other group's housewife uses brand Y. When asked to talk about the housewife, the two groups may describe her differently, exposing how they feel about the kind of people who buy brand X or Y. Advertisers hope to discover which brands appeal to what types of people this way.

Motivation researchers have found out that hot soup appeals to us not only because it tastes good, but because it means warmth,

☞ CURIOUS ADVERTISEMENT OF 100 YEARS AGO!!

PEARS' SOAP

PEARS' SOAP 1789.

gives com-plexions as vnto new milk and ripe cherries

Comely dames, brave squires, pretty little misses, & smart little masters, regularly use

PEARS' SOAP

Pears — Soapmaker to ye King
Pears' Soap can be bought at all ye shopps

As far back as the 1890s, advertisers knew that women did not buy soap just to make them clean, but to aid their youth and beauty as well. (New York Public Library Picture Collection)

comfort, and security. They learned that men bought cars not only because of economy, safety, or other sensible reasons, but because they liked cars with speed and power. They learned that women did not buy soap just to make them clean, but to promote their youth and beauty. They also learned that housewives would not buy cake mixes at first because they felt they were lazy if they did. The cake-mix makers solved the problem by changing the mix so that the housewife had to add fresh milk or eggs. Cake-mix sales then began rising.

Motivation research is still being done today, but you do not hear as much about it as you did in the 1950s and early 1960s, when it was a fad both for advertisers to use it and for many people to criticize it.

APPEALS AND TECHNIQUES

What must the advertiser do to get people to react appropriately to his advertising? The advertising must capture the *attention* of the audience. It must arouse *interest* in what is being offered. It must create a *desire* for the item. And it must make the person *act* at the appropriate time.

A key idea behind advertising is that people always have reasons for what they do. Sometimes people themselves are not aware of the reasons, but they still exist. Advertisers have learned to put their messages in terms of what *you* want instead of what *they* want you to do. This is called the *you* approach. It is the basis for advertising *appeals*, the reasons advertisers give for asking us to buy or vote or think or donate money the way they wish us to. Entire advertising campaigns costing millions of dollars are commonly built around a single advertising appeal. When you see a promise like "Green Farms Milk Tastes Better," you know that the advertiser would really like to say "Buy Green Farms Milk." But that would be foolish — he has to give you a good reason to buy his milk.

Appeals can be combined for greater effect. A coat may be advertised for protection against cold and wind, but also as being the latest in fashion. A headline for a cereal may be based on the need for a good breakfast, or it may be based on the fact that the cereal

68

You don't have to be Jewish

to love Levy's
real Jewish Rye

Some advertising people say that advertisements must appear to be personal or they simply will not work. (Doyle, Dane, Bernbach, Inc.)

is crackly, crunchy, and tastes good. Just about everyone would agree with the need for a good breakfast; it is the sensible, rational approach. Perhaps not everyone would agree that we should eat a cereal simply because it crunches and tastes good. That is something we simply *like to do*. It is an emotional appeal. Emotional appeals often help sell the product by suggesting that it will give the buyer emotional security, love, a sense of power, sexual attractiveness, prestige, a better self-image, or some other self-indulgent characteristic or feeling. Sometimes it does, but this technique is strongly attacked by critics of advertising.

One of the most important keys to effective advertising is finding a theme that will appeal to millions of people, yet one which each person will read as if it were directed to him or her alone. This is the reason some advertising people say that there is no such thing as mass communications: advertising must appear to be personal or it simply will not work.

To make the advertising more interesting, advertising people often use bright, catchy slogans, rhymes, jingles, and other devices that are remembered simply because they are so entertaining. You can probably sing a few popular jingles right this minute. One of America's most famous orchestras, the Boston Pops, made a long-playing record just of commercial jingle music.

Sometimes it is more important to make the slogan memorable than it is to give it a good appeal. The political slogan "I Like Ike," used during the 1952 presidential campaign, said nothing about General Dwight D. Eisenhower. However, it was almost impossible to forget the slogan and it may have helped the general win the election.

Suppose someone decides to do what an advertisement suggests. Usually he cannot do it immediately — he has to wait until he gets the chance. How do advertisers make sure he will remember?

Like electricity, we do not know exactly what memory is, but we do know a lot about how it works. We know that we learn and remember things that are closely connected with other things. This is the reason advertisers put the brand name of the product together with the type of product. Unless it is a very well-known brand or name, you do not see an advertisement for Foster — it is for Foster's Clothes. It is not Harold's — it is Harold's Furniture. After a while, you connect the two yourself.

Advertisers often try to get other key ideas remembered by connecting them with their name and product time after time. Lane's Brilliant Diamonds or Sim's Fine Clocks are examples. Sometimes the names themselves carry the main idea, as in Finetone Radios or Fursoft Slippers.

Repetition is another way to get something remembered. The more often we hear something, the better we remember it. This is one reason advertisers repeat commercials so often. Another reason is that we tend to remember the last things we see or hear.

People will more likely respond to advertising if they happen to need what is being offered anyway. But if the advertiser offers them something special, sometimes they can be persuaded to act a little faster or to try something they might not have bothered with. Coupons, for example, are very useful in getting people to try a new product or to switch to another brand. Coupons appear most frequently in newspapers, and the ten-cents-off coupon is the most popular.

72

Every mother's dream:
A cleancut American drain.

© 1969 Lehn & Fink

When crewcuts went out, cleancut American drains went with them.

A lot of the hair that used to wind up on the barber's floor is now winding up down your drains.

And there's nothing like a nest of hair to clog a drain.

That's why you need Down the Drain liquid drain opener.

It not only cuts soap and kitchen fats and grease. Down the Drain _even_ cuts hair.

Just pour it into your sluggish drains. Or, if worse has come to worst, right into the backed-up water.

Or, pour Down the Drain down your drains regularly and keep them clean and clear. It's either Down the Drain or back to crewcuts.

15¢ off on a haircut for your drains.

15¢ · 15¢

15¢ · 15¢

STORE COUPON

Some advertisements offer coupons. (Doyle, Dane, Bernbach, Inc., for Lehn & Fink)

HEY GANG, GET ON THE BRAVES BANDWAGON

Hank Aaron

FREE

BRAVES UNIFORM KIT

16 *Braves*

"A Pair of Numerals"

Braves "Chest Letters"

"Braves 'Laughing Indian' Arm Patch"

During Post Cereals Month you can get a free Braves Uniform Kit. Three kinds of permanent transfers you iron on. Just send in two box tops from Post Cereals to:
GENERAL FOODS, Box 4011, Kankakee, Illinois 60901. (Allow 6-8 weeks for delivery—offer good in month of August only.)

Get box tops from any of the following Post Cereals: Honeycomb® · Alpha-Bits® · Super Sugar Crisp® · Sugar Rice Krinkles® · Crispy Critters® · Raisin Bran® · Grape-Nuts® Bran & Prune Flakes® · Grape-Nuts Flakes® · Fortified Oat Flakes® · Post Toasties® · 40% Bran Flakes®

Reserved Seat Ticket To A Braves August Home Game ... Only 25¢ and Four Post Cereals Box Tops

During Post Cereals Month you can get a reserved seat to a Braves home game by sending in only 25¢ and four box tops from Post Cereals. Cut out the coupon and choose the game you want to see.

Aug. 8 Mets _____
Aug. 9 Mets _____
Aug. 10 Mets _____
Aug. 12 Phillies _____
Aug. 13 Phillies _____
Aug. 14 Phillies _____
Aug. 15 Cardinals _____
Aug. 16 Cardinals _____
Aug. 17 Cardinals _____
Aug. 29 Cubs _____
Aug. 30 Cubs _____
Aug. 31 Cubs _____

ATLANTA STADIUM

AUG. 12

Send four box tops and 25¢ handling charge for each ticket to: Post Ticket Offer "B", P.O. Box 4064, Atlanta, Ga. 30302. Indicate 1st, 2nd choice. Allow 10 days for delivery.

Name _____
Address _____
City _____
State _____ Zip _____

Many companies try to reach potential customers through their children. (The Post Cereals Division of the General Foods Corporation by Benton & Bowles, Inc.)

In addition, everything from informational booklets to free samples are offered by advertisers. Many of these offers involve filling in coupons from advertisements. People seem to enjoy clipping and filling out coupons. A small amount of money is sometimes requested to make sure that those who ask for information are really interested in the product. Offers of jewelry, glassware, toys, or other similar items are called *premiums*. A larger sum of money is usually asked for these items, but it is almost always less than what a person would have to pay for the same thing in a store. Often a box top or other *proof-of-purchase* is required.

Many companies try to reach potential customers through their children. One year General Electric offered a magic-ray gun and a space helmet to children who brought their mothers into stores that sold G.E. refrigerators. Recently, another company offered

74

a special children's coloring book — featuring a popular character — to mothers who came in to look at the company's carpets.

Some critics of advertising believe that advertising is making children into *consumer trainees* and that they are learning to be impulsive self-service shoppers. Many people do not believe this is true, however, and advertising to children continues to be a controversial matter. It is just one of the many criticisms that some people have of the entire advertising business.

HOW PEOPLE FEEL ABOUT ADVERTISING

In 1962 the American Association of Advertising Agencies, the best-known national advertising association, sponsored a research study to find out how people felt about advertising. Some of the best researchers in the country — including professors from Harvard University — worked on this study. Here are some of the things they found out.

Advertising was one of the top three items that people say they enjoy complaining about but do not take too seriously. (The other two were the federal government and clothing and fashions.)

However, fifteen of every hundred people do believe that advertising is one of the things most in need of immediate attention and change.

Do people feel favorable or unfavorable to advertising? Forty-one of every hundred felt favorable to advertising. Thirty-four percent had mixed feelings. Fourteen percent felt unfavorably. (There were always some people who had no opinion, so the scores do not always add up to 100 percent.)

When asked why people *should* feel favorable to advertising, 57 percent said the reason is that advertising is informative.

When asked why people should feel unfavorable to advertising, the three main reasons given were because of false or misleading advertising, because there is too much advertising, and because it interrupts entertainment.

76

IN MEMORY OF
THE 1,700,000 AMERICANS
WHO DIED FOR NOTHING

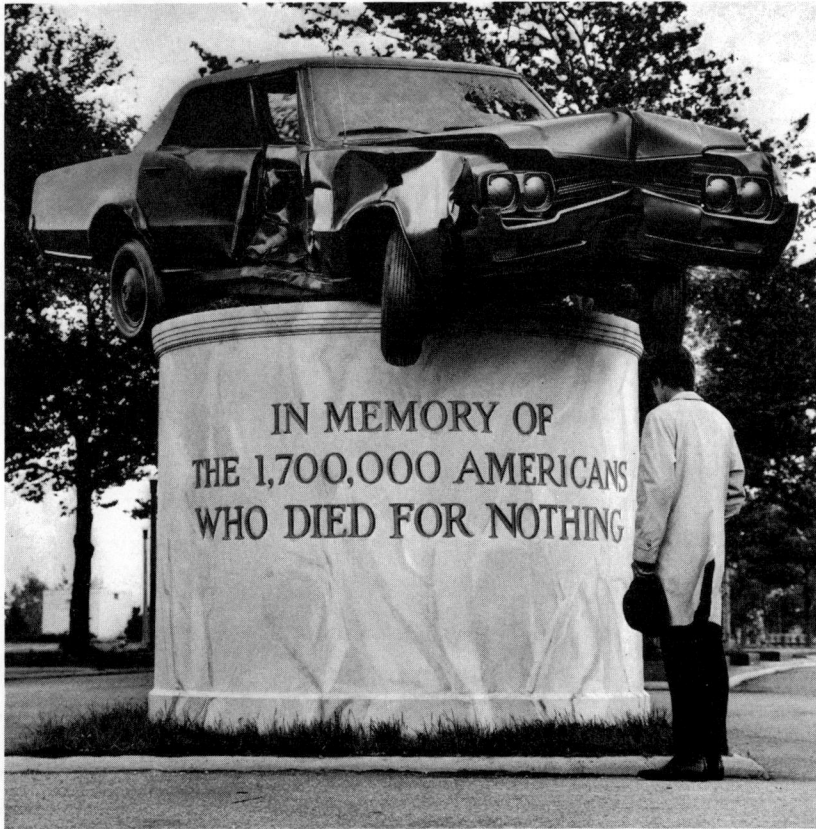

Here, at a time of remembrance, is our monument to the monumental folly of automobile drivers. Dead in a massacre that has taken 1,700,000 lives since 1900, and continues unabated today.

Think about it: The body count of Americans killed in action in all of America's wars since 1775 stands at 638,000. And in 69 short years, motorists have surpassed that stunning figure by over a million, men, women and children.

All of them dead.

Violently dead.

Agonizingly dead.

And for what?

For the sake of an extra martini?

For the thrill of passing a car on a blind curve at 67 miles an hour?

To save 15 seconds by jumping a light?

Before this year is over, one out of four cars in this country will be involved in an accident.

The lucky occupants will get a scare and go through the infuriating process of filling out all the insurance forms, getting repair estimates, and putting their cars up in a body shop for a few days.

They also won't get to where they were going in such a hurry.

All the other richpooroldyoung people will be dead (or wishing they were dead).

It doesn't have to happen to you.

But your protection won't start until you realize that it can happen to you: That, in less than a second, your car can be turned into a smoking hulk of broken glass and twisted steel.

That men with acetylene torches may have to cut your wife or kids out of it.

That flashing red lights and wailing sirens can come for you. Or yours.

That all you cherish (your life, or theirs; your well-being, or theirs) can be lost in that single instant.

Some people simply don't have the guts to imagine themselves in such anguish. Yet we're asking you to imagine it every time you get into your car. (If that sounds morbid, it's nothing compared to the possible alternative.) Because without a certain amount of healthy fear, there's no reason to do any of the things that can prevent the tragedy.

Like using your seatbelts. (They really do save lives, not to mention eyes, noses, and other personal possessions.)

Like the simple act of keeping a rag in the car for cleaning your windows and headlights. ("I never even saw him, officer.")

And having your brakes checked regularly, and replacing worn tires. And doing all the other little things you know about and don't bother about.

Aren't you worth the bother?

Please drive safely.

Mobil.
We want you to live.

© Mobil Oil Corporation

Some people said that advertising is informative. (Doyle, Dane, Bernbach, Inc., for Mobil Oil Corporation)

Is advertising essential to our economy? Seventy-eight percent agreed or partially agreed that it is.

Does advertising help result in better products? Seventy-four percent agreed or partially agreed that this is so.

Does advertising result in higher prices or lower prices? Only 40 percent believe that advertising results in lower prices. Forty-five percent believe that it results in higher prices.

Does advertising persuade people to buy things they should not? Sixty-five percent of the people agree or partially agree that it does.

Does advertising insult the intelligence of the average consumer? Forty-three percent say yes and the same percentage say no.

Does advertising generally present a true picture of the product? Fifty-three percent do not think so. Forty-one percent do.

One very important finding was that not everyone reacted the same way to the same advertising. What some people found stupid or annoying, others found entertaining.

Now let us take some of these criticisms and see how they are answered by those who defend advertising.

Criticism: "Too much money is spent on advertising. All that money should be spent on things we really need — like schools and hospitals."

Rebuttal: Advertising is big business, no question about it. In 1968, American industry spent 12 billion dollars on advertising. One popular defense of this tremendous expenditure is that if businesses were not permitted to advertise new products and services, they would not grow. They would not be able to invest in new businesses and research, jobs would not be created, and wages and salaries would fall. Since schools, hospitals, and other public services are supported by corporate and individual tax money, many people believe that advertising does contribute to the public welfare. They feel that advertising is needed for a dynamic, expanding economy also.

Criticism: "Advertising raises the cost of what we buy."

Rebuttal: True . . . sometimes. For a few kinds of products, advertising does raise the price substantially — about 25 percent for luxury items like cosmetics. However, for most of the day-to-day necessities, such as supermarket items, the additional cost is incredibly low — often less than a penny. In some cases, products would cost more without advertising. Why? Because advertising creates sales, and the more a manufacturer sells, the more products he can make. The more products he makes, the cheaper he can make them.

Criticism: "Maybe so, but advertising still makes people buy what they do not need."

Rebuttal: Many people believe this is so. In a way it is. After all, we do not really need much more than a cave to live in, an animal skin to wear, a hunk of raw meat and some berries, and maybe a fire. Prehistoric man lived that way for thousands of years. Do you really *need* that new dress? Or baseball glove? Try to convince your father he does not need his car. Tell your mother she does not need her vacuum cleaner — she could use a broom. What do you think they would say?

Criticism: "I still believe that advertising can manipulate large numbers of people."

Rebuttal: Advertising *can* get many people interested in a product. Unfortunately, it can also probably convince some of the fool-

79

ish ones to buy something against their best interests. For people on the whole, however, this is simply not true. There is an old saying that the worst thing for a bad product is good advertising. If a product does not measure up to what the advertiser has promised, it will not be bought again, no matter how hard the advertiser tries to sell it. Very few products are profitable if they are sold only once. Eighty to ninety of every hundred new products fail because consumers find them no better than what they already use. So consumers do not buy them again. In 1957, for example, the Ford Motor Company spent millions of dollars advertising the Edsel, a new car that was going to be shown for the first time. So much interest was generated that, on the first weekend the Edsel was shown, over 2½ million people rushed out to see it. They did not like the car. The sales program was a failure and the company had to stop making the car. That is something to remember the next time you hear about advertising's ability to brainwash people.

Criticism: "Advertising ought to perform some kind of public service in addition to its business function."

Rebuttal: It does. An organization called the Advertising Council, Inc., has created almost a hundred major advertising campaigns in the public interest. The media have contributed over 2½ million dollars' worth of free space and time *every year* to help these efforts. You will recognize some of the campaigns. Take Smokey the Bear, for example. Smokey helped cut forest fires in half with his reminders. Public-service campaigns helped increase the sale of United States Savings bonds, improve schools and double Parent-Teacher Association membership, and get four times the num-

This state, this country.

North and South, East and West,
Young and Old, Rich and Poor,
Jew and Gentile,
Black and White and Brown and Yellow and Red,
This town, this city, this state, this country
bleeds a little every day.

Open your heart.
Empty your hands.
And roll up your sleeves.
With The American Red Cross.

Roll up your sleeves.

advertising contributed for the public good

Advertising for the public interest. (Advertising Council, Inc.)

Only you can prevent forest fires.

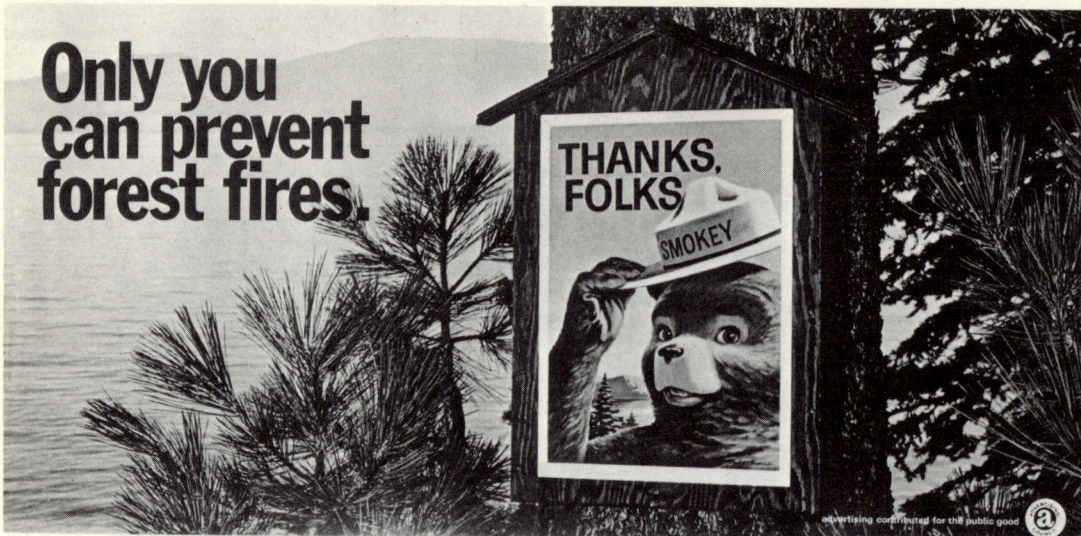

THANKS, FOLKS

SMOKEY

advertising contributed for the public good

ber of volunteers for the Peace Corps. The Keep America Beautiful and Equal Employment Opportunity campaigns were other advertising campaigns that benefit all of America.

Criticism: "There is no control over the kind of advertising that appears."

Rebuttal: There are advertising organizations that try to set fair standards and reduce the amount of objectionable advertising. The principal organization is the American Association of Advertising Agencies. All the media have standards that must be met also. The consumer is represented by the Better Business Bureaus and the Special Assistant for Consumer Affairs. About twenty federal administrative agencies have powers to regulate and control various advertising activities in the public interest. The most important agency is the Federal Trade Commission, which was given the power by Congress in 1938 to enforce a ban on false or misleading advertising. In cases where someone is deliberately trying to cheat the public, the FTC can immediately start legal action to see that the offender stops and is punished if necessary.

Other federal agencies that regulate advertising directly or indirectly are the Food and Drug Administration, which is primarily concerned with accurate labeling, and the Federal Communications Commission, which oversees all radio and television stations. The Securities and Exchange Commission has very strict rules about the advertising of corporate stock and other financial investments, and the U.S. Post Office has regulations prohibiting the use of mail for lotteries, fraud, and obscene literature.

As you can see, there are rebuttals for almost every criticism of advertising. Unfortunately, the problems are very complicated and people interpret the facts differently. While oversimplifying, we have tried to give you an idea of just some of the different interpretations and positions people take on the value and importance of advertising.

GLOSSARY

AGATE LINE — A space one column wide by $\frac{1}{14}$ of an inch deep. It is the unit of measurement in newspaper and magazine advertising.

AIDED RECALL — A post-test in which the interviewer gives some aids to the respondents to help them remember an advertisment.

BLEED — An illustration or part of an illustration that runs to the edge of a page.

CLASSIFIED ADVERTISING — Small ads, usually at the back of a newspaper or magazine, with small type and no illustrations and grouped by subject.

COMPREHENSIVE — A layout that includes a sketch of the illustration and the copywriter's headline lettered in the finished print size and type.

COOPERATIVE ADVERTISING — Advertising run by a dealer for a manufacturer's product, and for which the manufacturer pays part of the cost.

COPY — The words or text in an advertisement.

CREATIVE GROUP — A team of advertising agency staff members — including the copywriter, art director, and producer — that creates the ad.

DIRECT MAIL — Advertising sent through the mails.

DISPLAY ADVERTISING — Large ads that appear throughout a magazine or newspaper.

84

EARLY FRINGE — Television viewing time from 5:00 P.M. to 7:30 P.M. This viewing time comes just before prime time, the time of the largest viewing audience.

FILMOGRAPH — A film of storyboard sketches or still photographs of a commercial. Filmographs are shown to consumers to pre-test a commercial's effectiveness.

FREQUENCY — The number of times an advertising message reaches its audience.

INSTITUTIONAL ADVERTISING — Advertising that does not attempt to sell a company product or service, but does promote a company's image or ideas.

LATE FRINGE — Television viewing time from 11 P.M. to the time the station signs off the air.

MAKE-GOOD — The rerunning of an advertisement that a medium did not run correctly the first time. Because the medium is at fault, there is no extra charge to the advertiser.

MARKETING MIX — A combination of many methods of selling: advertising, personal selling, public relations, sales promotion, merchandising.

MEDIA; MASS MEDIA — Media, the plural of medium, is the method of communication by which advertising and other information is delivered. Mass media are the larger public information services, such as newspapers, magazines, radio, and television.

PIGGYBACKING — Running two or more commercials in a length of time normally bought for one.

POST-TEST — Tests given after the showing of an ad to measure its effectiveness.

85

PREPRINT — A page or section of advertisements printed separately from, or in advance of, a newspaper and inserted into the newspaper. It is often printed in color on a higher quality paper.

PRETEST — Showing or publishing advertising on a small scale before the campaign itself, to test its probable effectiveness.

PRIME TIME — The time during which a radio or TV station has the greatest number of listeners or viewers.

PURE RECALL — A post-test in which the interviewer gives no memory aids and asks the respondents to recall ads they saw.

REACH — The number of people who see or hear the advertising message.

STORYBOARD — A series of small sketches of a TV commercial to guide film or video-tape production workers.

THUMBNAILS — An art director's first small sketches of the illustrations to appear in an ad.

INDEX

88

90